FAVORITE
POEMS
for
BEDTIME

A CHILD'S COLLECTION

FOR MIA AND DAMON
May you have sweet dreams, always.

Published by Bushel & Peck Books, a family-run publishing house in Fresno, California, that believes in uplifting children with the highest standards of art, music, literature, and ideas. Find beautiful books for gifted young minds at www.bushelandpeckbooks.com.

Type set in Temeraire and Baskerville.

Designed by David Miles.

Bushel & Peck Books is dedicated to fighting illiteracy all over the world. For every book we sell, we donate one to a child in need—book for book. To nominate a school or organization to receive free books, please visit www.bushelandpeckbooks.com.

ISBN: 9781638190172

First Edition

Printed in the United States

10 9 8 7 6 5 4 3 2 1

FAVORITE
POEMS
for
BEDTIME

A CHILD'S COLLECTION

BUSHEL
& PECK
BOOKS

CONTENTS

MY SHADOW

Robert Louis Stevenson

I have a little shadow that goes in and out with me,
And what can be the use of him is more than I can see.
He is very, very like me from the heels up to the head;
And I see him jump before me, when I jump into my bed.

The funniest thing about him is the way he likes to grow—
Not at all like proper children, which is always very slow;
For he sometimes shoots up taller like an india-rubber ball,
And he sometimes gets so little that there's none of him at all.

He hasn't got a notion of how children ought to play,
And can only make a fool of me in every sort of way.
He stays so close beside me, he's a coward, you can see;
I'd think shame to stick to nursie as that shadow sticks to me!

One morning, very early, before the sun was up,
I rose and found the shining dew on every buttercup;

But my lazy little shadow, like an arrant sleepy-head,

Had stayed at home behind me and was fast asleep in bed.

IN A GARDEN

Algernon Charles Swinburne

Baby, see the flowers!
    —Baby sees
Fairer things than these,
        Fairer though they be than dreams of ours.

Baby, hear the birds!
    —Baby knows
Better songs than those,
        Sweeter though they sound than sweetest words.

Baby, see the moon!
    —Baby's eyes
Laugh to watch it rise,
        Answering light with love and night with noon.

Baby, hear the sea!
    —Baby's face

Takes a graver grace,
    Touched with wonder what the sound may be.

Baby, see the star!
    —Baby's hand
Opens, warm and bland,
    Calm in claim of all things fair that are.

Baby, hear the bells!
    —Baby's head
Bows, as ripe for bed,
    Now the flowers curl round and close their cells.

Baby, flower of light,
    Sleep, and see
Brighter dreams than we,
    Till good day shall smile away good night.

THE SUGAR-PLUM TREE

Eugene Field

Have you ever heard of the Sugar-Plum Tree?
'Tis a marvel of great renown!
It blooms on the shore of the Lollypop sea
In the garden of Shut-Eye Town;
The fruit that it bears is so wondrously sweet
(As those who have tasted it say)
That good little children have only to eat
Of that fruit to be happy next day.

When you've got to the tree, you would have a hard time
To capture the fruit which I sing;
The tree is so tall that no person could climb
To the boughs where the sugar-plums swing!
But up in that tree sits a chocolate cat,
And a gingerbread dog prowls below—
And this is the way you contrive to get at
Those sugar-plums tempting you so:

You say but the word to that gingerbread dog
And he barks with such terrible zest
That the chocolate cat is at once all agog,
As her swelling proportions attest.
And the chocolate cat goes cavorting around
From this leafy limb unto that,
And the sugar-plums tumble, of course, to the ground—
Hurrah for that chocolate cat!

There are marshmallows, gumdrops, and peppermint canes,
With stripings of scarlet or gold,
And you carry away of the treasure that rains,
As much as your apron can hold!
So come, little child, cuddle closer to me
In your dainty white nightcap and gown,
And I'll rock you away to that Sugar-Plum Tree
In the garden of Shut-Eye Town.

XXXVIII. (SLEEP)

Emily Dickinson

———

Sleep is supposed to be,
By souls of sanity,
The shutting of the eye.

Sleep is the station grand
Down which on either hand
The hosts of witness stand!

Morn is supposed to be,
By people of degree,
The breaking of the day.

Morning has not occurred!
That shall aurora be
East of eternity;

One with the banner gay,
One in the red array, —
That is the break of day.

STOPPING BY WOODS ON A SNOWY EVENING

Robert Frost

Whose woods these are I think I know.
His house is in the village though;
He will not see me stopping here
To watch his woods fill up with snow.

My little horse must think it queer
To stop without a farmhouse near
Between the woods and frozen lake
The darkest evening of the year.

He gives his harness bells a shake
To ask if there is some mistake.
The only other sound's the sweep
Of easy wind and downy flake.

The woods are lovely, dark and deep,

But I have promises to keep,

And miles to go before I sleep,

And miles to go before I sleep.

SO, SO, ROCK-A-BY SO!

Eugene Field

So, so, rock-a-by so!
Off to the garden where dreamikins grow;
And here is a kiss on your winkyblink eyes,
    And here is a kiss on your dimpledown cheek
And here is a kiss for the treasure that lies
In the beautiful garden way up in the skies
    Which you seek.
Now mind these three kisses wherever you go—
So, so, rock-a-by so!
There's one little fumfay who lives there, I know,
For he dances all night where the dreamikins grow;
I send him this kiss on your droopydrop eyes,
    I send him this kiss on your rosy-red cheek.
And here is a kiss for the dream that shall rise
When the fumfay shall dance in those far-away skies
    Which you seek.

Be sure that you pay those three kisses you owe—
So, so, rock-a-by so!
And, by-low, as you rock-a-by go,
Don't forget mother who loveth you so!
And here is her kiss on your weepydeep eyes,
    And here is her kiss on your peachypink cheek,
And here is her kiss for the dreamland that lies
Like a babe on the breast of those far-away skies
    Which you seek—
The blinkywink garden where dreamikins grow—
So, so, rock-a-by so!

II. (OUR SHARE OF NIGHT TO BEAR)

Emily Dickinson

Our share of night to bear,
Our share of morning,
Our blank in bliss to fill,
Our blank in scorning.

Here a star, and there a star,
Some lose their way.
Here a mist, and there a mist,
Afterwards — day!

A PAPER MOON

Annette Wynne

A paper moon, I'll hang it high
Up in a dark blue paper sky;
Some pretty silvery stars I'll make—
All for the little lone moon's sake;
My bed shall be the evening grass,
Where only fairy people pass;
　　Where no one sees
　　But the breeze
　　That hurries lightly through the trees;
The sky I'll hang above my head,
When I'm undressed to go to bed;
And so, a gypsy child I'll play
That has no real home to stay.

TWINKLE, TWINKLE, LITTLE STAR

Jane Taylor

Twinkle, twinkle, little star,
How I wonder what you are!
Up above the world so high,
Like a diamond in the sky.

When the blazing sun is gone,
When he nothing shines upon,
Then you show your little light,
Twinkle, twinkle, all the night.

Then the trav'ller in the dark,
Thanks you for your tiny spark,
He could not see which way to go,
If you did not twinkle so.

In the dark blue sky you keep,

And often thro' my curtains peep,

For you never shut your eye,

Till the sun is in the sky.

'Tis your bright and tiny spark,

Lights the trav'ller in the dark,

Tho' I know not what you are,

Twinkle, twinkle, little star.

LITTLE BOY BLUE

Eugene Field

The little toy dog is covered with dust,
  But sturdy and stanch he stands;
And the little toy soldier is red with rust,
  And the musket moulds in his hands.
Time was when the little toy dog was new,
  And the soldier was passing fair;
And that was the time when our Little Boy Blue
  Kissed them and put them there.

"Now, don't you go till I come," he said,
  "And don't you make any noise!"
So, toddling off to his trundle-bed,
  He dreamt of the pretty toys;
And, as he was dreaming, an angel song
  Awakened our Little Boy Blue—
Oh! the years are many, the years are long,
  But the little toy friends are true!

Aye, faithful to Little Boy Blue they stand,
  Each in the same old place—
Awaiting the touch of a little hand,
  The smile of a little face;
And they wonder, as waiting the long years through
  In the dust of that little chair,
What has become of our Little Boy Blue,
  Since he kissed them and put them there.

WEE WILLIE WINKIE

William Miller

Wee Willie Winkie rins through the town,
Up-stairs and doon-stairs, in his nicht-gown,
Tirlin' at the window, cryin' at the lock,
"Are the weans in their bed?—for it's now ten o'clock."

Hey, Willie Winkie! are ye comin' ben?
The cat's singin' gay thrums to the sleepin' hen,
The doug's speldered on the floor, and disna gie a cheep;
But here's a waukrife laddie that winna fa' asleep.

Onything but sleep, ye rogue! glow'rin' like the moon,
Rattlin' in an airn jug wi' an airn spoon,
Rumblin' tumblin' roun' about, crowin' like a cock,
Skirlin' like a kenna-what—wauknin' sleepin' folk.

Hey, Willie Winkie! the wean's in a creel!
Waumblin' aff a body's knee like a vera eel,

Ruggin' at the cat's lug, and ravellin' a' her thrums,—
Hey, Willie Winkie!—See, there he comes!

Wearie is the mither that has a storie wean,
A wee stumpie stoussie that canna rin his lane,
That has a battle aye wi' sleep before he'll close an ee;
But a kiss frae aff his rosy lips gies strength anew to me.

THE SEA OF SUNSET

Emily Dickinson

This is the land the sunset washes,
These are the banks of the Yellow Sea;
Where it rose, or whither it rushes,
These are the western mystery!

Night after night her purple traffic
Strews the landing with opal bales;
Merchantmen poise upon horizons,
Dip, and vanish with fairy sails.

BEHIND EACH STAR

Annette Wynne

Behind each star a small dream hides
But will not show its head,
Unless you're very, very good—
And fast asleep in bed.

A DREAM

William Blake

Once a dream did wave a shade
O'er my angel-guarded bed,
That an emmet lost its way
When on grass methought I lay.

Troubled, 'wildered, and forlorn,
Dark, benighted, travel-worn,
Over many a tangled spray,
All heart-broke, I heard her say:

"Oh, my children! do they cry?
Do they hear their father sigh?
Now they look abroad to see.
Now return and weep for me."

Pitying, I dropped a tear;
But I saw a glow-worm near,

Who replied, "What wailing wight
Calls the watchman of the night?

"I am set to light the ground
While the beetle goes his round.
Follow now the beetle's hum—
Little wanderer, hie thee home!"

THE OWL AND THE PUSSY-CAT

Edward Lear

The Owl and the Pussy-Cat went to sea
    In a beautiful pea-green boat;
They took some honey, and plenty of money
    Wrapped up in a five-pound note.
The Owl looked up to the moon above,
    And sang to a small guitar,
"O lovely Pussy! O Pussy, my love!
    What a beautiful Pussy you are,—
        You are,
    What a beautiful Pussy you are!"

Pussy said to the Owl, "You elegant fowl!
    How wonderful sweet you sing!
Oh, let us be married,—too long we have tarried,—
    But what shall we do for a ring?"

They sailed away for a year and a day
    To the land where the Bong-tree grows,
And there in a wood a piggy-wig stood
    With a ring in the end of his nose,—
      His nose,
    With a ring in the end of his nose.

"Dear Pig, are you willing to sell for one shilling
    Your ring?" Said the piggy, "I will,"
So they took it away, and were married next day
    By the turkey who lives on the hill.
They dined upon mince and slices of quince,
    Which they ate with a runcible spoon,
And hand in hand on the edge of the sand
    They danced by the light of the moon,—
      The moon,
    They danced by the light of the moon.

IF I HAD BUT TWO LITTLE WINGS

Samuel T. Coleridge

If I had but two little wings
    And were a little feathery bird,
        To you I'd fly, my dear!
But thoughts like these are idle things
    And I stay here.

But in my sleep to you I fly:
    I'm always with you in my sleep!
        The world is all one's own.
And then one wakes, and where am I?
    All, all alone.

A FAREWELL

Charles Kingsley

My fairest child, I have no song to give you;
    No lark could pipe to skies so dull and gray;
Yet, ere we part, one lesson I can leave you
    For every day.

Be good, sweet maid, and let who will be clever;
    Do noble things, not dream them all day long:
And so make life, death, and that vast forever
    One grand, sweet song.

WYNKEN, BLYNKEN, AND NOD

Eugene Field

Wynken, Blynken, and Nod one night
    Sailed off in a wooden shoe,—
Sailed on a river of crystal light
    Into a sea of dew.
"Where are you going, and what do you wish?"
    The old moon asked the three.
"We have come to fish for the herring-fish
    That live in this beautiful sea;
    Nets of silver and gold have we,"
        Said Wynken,
        Blynken,
        And Nod.

The old moon laughed and sang a song,
    As they rocked in the wooden shoe;

And the wind that sped them all night long
    Ruffled the waves of dew;
The little stars were the herring-fish
    That lived in the beautiful sea.
"Now cast your nets wherever you wish,—
    Never afeard are we!"
    So cried the stars to the fishermen three,
        Wynken,
        Blynken,
        And Nod.

All night long their nets they threw
    To the stars in the twinkling foam,—
Then down from the skies came the wooden shoe,
    Bringing the fishermen home:
'Twas all so pretty a sail, it seemed
    As if it could not be;
And some folk thought 'twas a dream they'd dreamed
    Of sailing that beautiful sea;
    But I shall name you the fishermen three:
        Wynken,
        Blynken,
        And Nod.

Wynken and Blynken are two little eyes,
  And Nod is a little head,
And the wooden shoe that sailed the skies
  Is a wee one's trundle-bed;
So shut your eyes while Mother sings
  Of wonderful sights that be,
And you shall see the beautiful things
    As you rock on the misty sea
    Where the old shoe rocked the fishermen three,
      Wynken,
      Blynken,
      And Nod.

PIPPA

An excerpt from Pippa Passes *by Robert Browning*

The year's at the spring,
The day's at the morn;
Morning's at seven;
The hillside's dew pearled;

The lark's on the wing;
The snail's on the thorn;
God's in His heaven—
All's right with the world!

THE CAPTAIN'S DAUGHTER

James T. Fields

We were crowded in the cabin,
　　Not a soul would dare to sleep,—
It was midnight on the waters,
　　And a storm was on the deep.

'Tis a fearful thing in winter
　　To be shattered by the blast,
And to hear the rattling trumpet
　　Thunder, "Cut away the mast!"

So we shuddered there in silence,—
　　For the stoutest held his breath,
While the hungry sea was roaring
　　And the breakers talked with Death.

As thus we sat in darkness,
    Each one busy with his prayers,
"We are lost!" the captain shouted
    As he staggered down the stairs.

But his little daughter whispered,
    As she took his icy hand,
"Isn't God upon the ocean,
    Just the same as on the land?"

Then we kissed the little maiden.
    And we spoke in better cheer,
And we anchored safe in harbour
    When the morn was shining clear.

THE NIGHTINGALE

William Cowper

A nightingale, that all day long
Had cheered the village with his song,
Nor yet at eve his note suspended,
Nor yet when eventide was ended,
Began to feel, as well he might,
The keen demands of appetite;
When, looking eagerly around,
He spied far off, upon the ground,
A something shining in the dark,
And knew the glow-worm by his spark;
So, stooping down from hawthorn top,
He thought to put him in his crop.
The worm, aware of his intent,
Harangued him thus, right eloquent:
"Did you admire my lamp," quoth he,
"As much as I your minstrelsy,

You would abhor to do me wrong,

As much as I to spoil your song;

For 'twas the self-same power divine,

Taught you to sing and me to shine;

That you with music, I with light,

Might beautify and cheer the night."

The songster heard his short oration,

And warbling out his approbation,

Released him, as my story tells,

And found a supper somewhere else.

THE OWL

Alfred, Lord Tennyson

When cats run home and light is come,
　　And dew is cold upon the ground,
And the far-off stream is dumb,
　　And the whirring sail goes round,
　　And the whirring sail goes round;
　　　Alone and warming his five wits,
　　　The white owl in the belfry sits.

When merry milkmaids click the latch,
　　And rarely smells the new-mown hay,
And the cock hath sung beneath the thatch
　　Twice or thrice his roundelay,
　　Twice or thrice his roundelay;
　　　Alone and warming his five wits,
　　　The white owl in the belfry sits.

HEAVEN IS NOT REACHED AT A SINGLE BOUND

An excerpt by J. G. Holland

———

Heaven is not reached at a single bound,
    But we build the ladder by which we rise
    From the lowly earth to the vaulted skies,
And we mount to its summit round by round.

I count this thing to be grandly true:
    That a noble deed is a step toward God,—
    Lifting the soul from the common clod
To a purer air and a broader view.

SONG OF LIFE

Charles Mackay

A traveller on a dusty road
    Strewed acorns on the lea;
And one took root and sprouted up,
    And grew into a tree.
Love sought its shade at evening-time,
    To breathe its early vows;
And Age was pleased, in heights of noon,
    To bask beneath its boughs.
The dormouse loved its dangling twigs,
    The birds sweet music bore—
It stood a glory in its place,
    A blessing evermore.
A little spring had lost its way
    Amid the grass and fern;
A passing stranger scooped a well
    Where weary men might turn.

He walled it in, and hung with care
    A ladle on the brink;
He thought not of the deed he did,
    But judged that Toil might drink.
He passed again; and lo! the well,
    By summer never dried,
Had cooled ten thousand parchéd tongues,
    And saved a life beside.
A nameless man, amid the crowd
    That thronged the daily mart,
Let fall a word of hope and love,
    Unstudied from the heart,
A whisper on the tumult thrown,
    A transitory breath,
It raised a brother from the dust,
    It saved a soul from death.
O germ! O fount! O word of love!
    O thought at random cast!
Ye were but little at the first,
    But mighty at the last.

FAIRY SONG

John Keats

Shed no tear! O shed no tear!
The flower will bloom another year.
Weep no more! O, weep no more!
Young buds sleep in the root's white core.
Dry your eyes! Oh! dry your eyes!
For I was taught in Paradise
To ease my breast of melodies—
      Shed no tear.

Overhead! look overhead!
'Mong the blossoms white and red—
Look up, look up. I flutter now
On this flush pomegranate bough.
See me! 'tis this silvery bell
Ever cures the good man's ill.
Shed no tear! O, shed no tear!

The flowers will bloom another year.
Adieu, adieu—I fly, adieu,
I vanish in the heaven's blue—
Adieu, adieu!

THE DAFFODIL

William Wordsworth

I wandered lonely as a cloud
    That floats on high o'er vales and hills,
When all at once I saw a crowd,
    A host of golden daffodils:
Beside the lake, beneath the trees,
Fluttering and dancing in the breeze.

Continuous as the stars that shine
    And twinkle on the milky way,
They stretched in never-ending line
    Along the margin of a bay;
Ten thousand saw I at a glance,
Tossing their heads in sprightly dance.

The waves beside them danced, but they
    Outdid the sparkling waves in glee:—

A poet could not but be gay

    In such a jocund company;

I gazed—and gazed—but little thought

What wealth the show to me had brought.

For oft, when on my couch I lie

    In vacant or in pensive mood,

They flash upon that inward eye

    Which is the bliss of solitude;

And then my heart with pleasure fills,

And dances with the daffodils.

A PAPER MOON

Annette Wynne

I think I'd like you better, Star,
If you were not so high and far,
So many friendly things are found
Quite near the ground.
I wonder if I saw you near
Would you appear
So very fine; I hope you would
Be just as pretty, bright, and good—
Not like some that only are
Fine and true when seen from afar.

I have a little candle light,
Friendly, simple, good and bright,—
I love it for it shines at night
Upon the stairs
And waits, still shining, till my prayers
Are said

And I'm about to jump to bed;
I say, "Good-night,
Dear candle light."

I think I'd like you better, Star,
If you were only not so far.

THE WIND AND THE MOON

George Macdonald

Said the Wind to the Moon, "I will blow you out,
>> You stare
>> In the air
>> Like a ghost in a chair,
> Always looking what I am about—
> I hate to be watched; I'll blow you out."

The Wind blew hard, and out went the Moon.
>> So, deep
>> On a heap
>> Of clouds to sleep,
> Down lay the Wind, and slumbered soon,
> Muttering low, "I've done for that Moon."

He turned in his bed; she was there again!

On high
In the sky,
With her one ghost eye,
The Moon shone white and alive and plain.
Said the Wind, "I will blow you out again."

The Wind blew hard, and the Moon grew dim.
"With my sledge,
And my wedge,
I have knocked off her edge!
If only I blow right fierce and grim,
The creature will soon be dimmer than dim."

He blew and he blew, and she thinned to a thread.
"One puff
More's enough
To blow her to snuff!
One good puff more where the last was bred,
And glimmer, glimmer, glum will go the thread."

He blew a great blast, and the thread was gone
In the air
Nowhere
Was a moonbeam bare;

Far off and harmless the shy stars shone—
Sure and certain the Moon was gone!

The Wind he took to his revels once more;
      On down,
      In town,
      Like a merry-mad clown,
He leaped and hallooed with whistle and roar—
"What's that?" The glimmering thread once more!

He flew in a rage—he danced and blew;
      But in vain
      Was the pain
      Of his bursting brain;
For still the broader the Moon-scrap grew,
The broader he swelled his big cheeks and blew.

Slowly she grew—till she filled the night,
      And shone
      On her throne
      In the sky alone,
A matchless, wonderful silvery light,
Radiant and lovely, the queen of the night.

Said the Wind: "What a marvel of power am I
    With my breath,
    Good faith!
    I blew her to death—
First blew her away right out of the sky—
Then blew her in; what strength have I!"

But the Moon she knew nothing about the affair;
    For high
    In the sky,
    With her one white eye,
Motionless, miles above the air,
She had never heard the great Wind blare.

THE SHUT-EYE TRAIN

Eugene Field

Come, my little one, with me!
There are wondrous sights to see
    As the evening shadows fall;
    In your pretty cap and gown,
        Don't detain
        The Shut-Eye train—
    "Ting-a-ling!" the bell it goeth,
    "Toot-toot!" the whistle bloweth,
And we hear the warning call:
"All aboard for Shut-Eye Town!"

Over hill and over plain
Soon will speed the Shut-Eye train!
    Through the blue where bloom the stars
    And the Mother Moon looks down
        We'll away
        To land of Fay—

Oh, the sights that we shall see there!
Come, my little one, with me there—
'Tis a goodly train of cars—
All aboard for Shut-Eye Town!

Swifter than a wild bird's flight,
Through the realms of fleecy light
We shall speed and speed away!
Let the Night in envy frown—
What care we
How wroth she be!
To the Balow-land above us,
To the Balow-folk who love us,
Let us hasten while we may—
All aboard for Shut-Eye Town!

HOW SLEEP THE BRAVE

William Collins

How sleep the brave, who sink to rest
By all their country's wishes blest!
When Spring, with dewy fingers cold,
Returns to deck their hallow'd mould,
She there shall dress a sweeter sod
Than Fancy's feet have ever trod.

By fairy hands their knell is rung,
By forms unseen their dirge is sung:
There Honour comes, a pilgrim gray,
To bless the turf that wraps their clay;
And Freedom shall a while repair
To dwell a weeping hermit there!

ABIDE WITH ME

Henry Francis Lyte

Abide with me! fast falls the eventide;
The darkness deepens; Lord, with me abide!
When other helpers fail, and comforts flee,
Help of the helpless, O abide with me.

Swift to its close ebbs out life's little day;
Earth's joys grow dim, its glories pass away;
Change and decay in all around I see:
O Thou who changest not, abide with me!

CROSSING THE BAR

Alfred, Lord Tennyson

Sunset and evening star,
      And one clear call for me!
And may there be no moaning of the bar,
      When I put out to sea,

But such a tide as moving seems asleep,
      Too full for sound and foam,
When that which drew from out the boundless deep
      Turns again home.

Twilight and evening bell,
      And after that the dark!
And may there be no sadness of farewell,
      When I embark;

For tho' from out our bourne of Time and Place
      The flood may bear me far,

I hope to see my Pilot face to face
When I have cross'd the bar.

LEAD, KINDLY LIGHT

John Henry Newman

Lead, kindly Light, amid th' encircling gloom,
Lead Thou me on,
The night is dark, and I am far from home,
Lead Thou me on.
Keep Thou my feet; I do not ask to see
The distant scene; one step enough for me.

I was not ever thus, nor prayed that Thou
Shouldst lead me on;
I loved to choose and see my path; but now
Lead Thou me on.
I loved the garish day; and, spite of fears,
Pride ruled my will: remember not past years.

So long Thy power hath blest me, sure it still
Will lead me on
O'er moor and fen, o'er crag and torrent, till

The night is gone,
And with the morn those angel faces smile,
Which I have loved long since, and lost a while.

THE LIGHT OF OTHER DAYS

Thomas Moore

———

Oft in the stilly night
 Ere slumber's chain has bound me,
Fond Memory brings the light
 Of other days around me:
  The smiles, the tears
  Of boyhood's years,
 The words of love then spoken;
  The eyes that shone,
  Now dimmed and gone,
 The cheerful hearts now broken!
Thus in the stilly night
 Ere slumber's chain has bound me,
Sad Memory brings the light
 Of other days around me.

When I remember all
    The friends so link'd together
I've seen around me fall
    Like leaves in wintry weather,
        I feel like one
        Who treads alone
    Some banquet-hall deserted,
        Whose lights are fled,
        Whose garlands dead,
    And all but he departed!
Thus in the stilly night
    Ere slumber's chain has bound me,
Sad Memory brings the light
    Of other days around me.

POLONIUS'S ADVICE

An excerpt from "Hamlet" by Shakespeare

See thou character. Give thy thoughts no tongue,
Nor any unproportion'd thought his act.
Be thou familiar, but by no means vulgar:
The friends thou hast, and their adoption tried,
Grapple them to thy soul with hoops of steel;
But do not dull thy palm with entertainment
Of each new-hatch'd, unfledg'd comrade. Beware
Of entrance to a quarrel; but, being in,
Bear 't that th' opposed may beware of thee.
Give every man thine ear, but few thy voice:
Take each man's censure, but reserve thy judgment.
Costly thy habit as thy purse can buy
But not expressed in fancy; rich, not gaudy:
For the apparel oft proclaims the man.
Neither a borrower nor a lender be;
For loan oft loses both itself and friend,

And borrowing dulls the edge of husbandry.

This above all: to thine own self be true;

And it must follow, as the night the day,

Thou canst not then be false to any man.

SLEEP, BABY, SLEEP

Elizabeth Prentiss

Sleep, baby, sleep!
Thy father's watching the sheep,
Thy mother's shaking the dreamland tree,
And down drops a little dream for thee.
Sleep, baby, sleep!

Sleep, baby, sleep!
The large stars are the sheep,
The little stars are the lambs, I guess,
The bright moon is the shepherdess.
Sleep, baby, sleep!

Sleep, baby, sleep!
Thy Savior loves His sheep;
He is the Lamb of God on high
Who for our sakes came down to die.
Sleep, baby, sleep!

XVII. (I NEVER SAW A MOOR)

Emily Dickinson

I never saw a moor,
I never saw the sea;
Yet know I how the heather looks,
And what a wave must be.

I never spoke with God,
Nor visited in heaven;
Yet certain am I of the spot
As if the chart were given.

PSALM OF THE DAY

Emily Dickinson

A something in a summer's day,
As slow her flambeaux burn away,
Which solemnizes me.

A something in a summer's noon, —
An azure depth, a wordless tune,
Transcending ecstasy.

And still within a summer's night
A something so transporting bright,
I clap my hands to see;

Then veil my too inspecting face,
Lest such a subtle, shimmering grace
Flutter too far for me.
The wizard-fingers never rest,
The purple brook within the breast

Still chafes its narrow bed;

Still rears the East her amber flag,
Guides still the sun along the crag
His caravan of red,

Like flowers that heard the tale of dews,
But never deemed the dripping prize
Awaited their low brows;

Or bees, that thought the summer's name
Some rumor of delirium
No summer could for them;

Or Arctic creature, dimly stirred
By tropic hint, — some travelled bird
Imported to the wood;

Or wind's bright signal to the ear,
Making that homely and severe,
Contented, known, before
The heaven unexpected came,
To lives that thought their worshipping
A too presumptuous psalm.

ROCK ME TO SLEEP

Elizabeth Akers Allen

Backward, turn backward, O time, in your flight,
Make me a child again just for tonight!
Mother, come back from the echoless shore,
Take me again to your heart as of yore;
Kiss from my forehead the furrows of care,
Smooth the few silver threads out of my hair;
Over my slumbers your loving watch keep;—
Rock me to sleep, mother, rock me to sleep.

Backward, flow backward, O tide of the years!
I am so weary of toil and of tears,—
Toil without recompense, tears all in vain,—
Take them, and give me my childhood again!
I have grown weary of dust and decay,—
Weary of flinging my soul-wealth away;
Weary of sowing for others to reap;—
Rock me to sleep, mother, rock me to sleep.

Tired of the hollow, the base, the untrue,
Mother, O mother, my heart calls for you!
Many a summer the grass has grown green,
Blossomed and faded, our faces between;
Yet with strong yearning and passionate pain
Long I to-night for your presence again.
Come from the silence so long and so deep;—
Rock me to sleep, mother, rock me to sleep.

Over my heart, in the days that are flown,
No love like mother-love ever has shone;
No other worship abides and endures—
Faithful, unselfish and patient, like yours;
None like a mother can charm away pain
From the sick soul and the world-weary brain.
Slumber's soft calms o'er my heavy lids creep;—
Rock me to sleep, mother, rock me to sleep.

Come, let your brown hair, just lighted with gold,
Fall on your shoulders again as of old;
Let it drop over my forehead to-night,
Shading my faint eyes away from the light;

For with its sunny-edged shadows once more
Haply will throng the sweet visions of yore;
Lovingly, softly, its bright billows sweep;—
Rock me to sleep, mother, rock me to sleep.

Mother, dear mother, the years have been long
Since I last listened your lullaby song;
Sing, then, and unto my soul it shall seem
Womanhood's years have been only a dream.
Clasped to your breast in a loving embrace,
With your light lashes just sweeping my face,
Never hereafter to wake or to weep;—
Rock me to sleep, mother, rock me to sleep.

AN ANSWER TO "ROCK ME TO SLEEP"

Unknown, from Poems Teachers Ask For

———

My child, ah, my child; thou art weary to-night,
Thy spirit is sad, and dim is the light;
Thou wouldst call me back from the echoless shore
To the trials of life, to thy heart as of yore;
Thou longest again for my fond loving care,
For my kiss on thy cheek, for my hand on thy hair;
But angels around thee their loving watch keep,
And angels, my darling, will rock thee to sleep.

"Backward?" Nay, onward, ye swift rolling years!
Gird on thy armor, keep back thy tears;
Count not thy trials nor efforts in vain,
They'll bring thee the light of thy childhood again.
Thou shouldst not weary, my child, by the way,

But watch for the light of that brighter day;
Not tired of "Sowing for others to reap,"
For angels, my darling, will rock thee to sleep.

Tired, my child, of the "base, the untrue!"
I have tasted the cup they have given to you;
I've felt the deep sorrow in the living green
Of a low mossy grave by the silvery stream.
But the dear mother I then sought for in vain
Is an angel presence and with me again;
And in the still night, from the silence deep,
Come the bright angels to rock me to sleep.

Nearer thee now than in days that are flown,
Purer the love-light encircling thy home;
Far more enduring the watch for tonight
Than ever earth worship away from the light;
Soon the dark shadows will linger no more.
Nor come to thy call from the opening door;
But know thou, my child, that the angels watch keep,
And soon, very soon, they'll rock thee to sleep.

They'll sing thee to sleep with a soothing song;
And, waking, thou'lt be with a heavenly throng;

And thy life, with its toil and its tears and pain,

Thou wilt then see has not been in vain.

Thou wilt meet those in bliss whom on earth thou didst love,

And whom thou hast taught of the "Mansions above."

"Never hereafter to suffer or weep,"

The angels, my darling, will rock thee to sleep.

WISHING

William Allingham

Ring-Ting! I wish I were a Primrose,
A bright yellow Primrose, blowing in the spring!
The stooping boughs above me,
The wandering bee to love me,
The fern and moss to creep across,
And the Elm tree for our king!

Nay—stay! I wish I were an Elm tree,
A great, lofty Elm tree, with green leaves gay!
The winds would set them dancing,
The sun and moonshine glance in,
The birds would house among the boughs,
And sweetly sing.

Oh no! I wish I were a Robin,
A Robin or a little Wren, everywhere to go;

Through forest, field, or garden,
And ask no leave or pardon,
Till winter comes with icy thumbs
To ruffle up our wing!

Well—tell! Where should I fly to,
Where go to sleep in the dark wood or dell?
Before a day was over,
Home comes the rover.
For mother's kiss—sweeter this
Than any other thing.

LADY BUTTON-EYES

Eugene Field

When the busy day is done,
And my weary little one
Rocketh gently to and fro;
When the night winds softly blow,
And the crickets in the glen
Chirp and chirp and chirp again;
When upon the haunted green
Fairies dance around their queen—
Then from yonder misty skies
Cometh Lady Button-Eyes.

Through the murk and mist and gloam
To our quiet, cozy home,
Where to singing, sweet and low,
Rocks a cradle to and fro;
Where the clock's dull monotone

Telleth of the day that's done;
Where the moonbeams hover o'er
Playthings sleeping on the floor—
Where my weary wee one lies
Cometh Lady Button-Eyes.

Cometh like a fleeting ghost
From some distant eerie coast;
Never footfall can you hear
As that spirit fareth near—
Never whisper, never word
From that shadow-queen is heard.
In ethereal raiment dight,
From the realm of fay and sprite
In the depth of yonder skies
Cometh Lady Button-Eyes.

Layeth she her hands upon
My dear weary little one,
And those white hands overspread
Like a veil the curly head,
Seem to fondle and caress
Every little silken tress;
Then she smooths the eyelids down

Over those two eyes of brown—
In such soothing, tender wise
Cometh Lady Button-Eyes.
Dearest, feel upon your brow
That caressing magic now;
For the crickets in the glen
Chirp and chirp and chirp again,
While upon the haunted green
Fairies dance around their queen,
And the moonbeams hover o'er
Playthings sleeping on the floor—
Hush, my sweet! from yonder skies
Cometh Lady Button-Eyes!

PLAYMATES

Emily Dickinson

========

God permits industrious angels
Afternoons to play.
I met one, — forgot my school-mates,
All, for him, straightway.

God calls home the angels promptly
At the setting sun;
I missed mine. How dreary marbles,
After playing Crown!

THE FOUNTAIN

James Russell Lowell

Into the sunshine,
    Full of the light,
Leaping and flashing
    From morn till night;

Into the moonlight,
    Whiter than snow,
Waving so flower-like
    When the winds blow;

Into the starlight
    Rushing in spray,
Happy at midnight,
    Happy by day;

Ever in motion,
    Blithesome and cheery,

Still climbing heavenward,
    Never aweary;

Glad of all weathers,
    Still seeming best,
Upward or downward,
    Motion thy rest;

Full of a nature
    Nothing can tame,
Changed every moment,
    Ever the same;

Ceaseless aspiring,
    Ceaseless content,
Darkness or sunshine
    Thy element;

Glorious fountain,
    Let my heart be
Fresh, changeful, constant,
    Upward, like thee!

SWEET AND LOW

Alfred, Lord Tennyson

Sweet and low, sweet and low,
    Wind of the western sea,
Low, low, breathe and blow,
    Wind of the western sea!
Over the rolling waters go,
    Come from the dropping moon and blow,
Blow him again to me;
    While my little one, while my pretty one sleeps.

Sleep and rest, sleep and rest,
    Father will come to thee soon;
Rest, rest, on mother's breast,
    Father will come to thee soon;
Father will come to his babe in the nest,
    Silver sails all out of the west
Under the silver moon:
    Sleep, my little one, sleep, my pretty one, sleep.

HOW MANY SECONDS IN A MINUTE?

Christina G. Rossetti

How many seconds in a minute?
    Sixty, and no more in it.
How many minutes in an hour?
    Sixty for sun and shower.
How many hours in a day?
    Twenty-four for work and play.
How many days in a week?
    Seven both to hear and speak.
How many weeks in a month?
    Four, as the swift moon runn'th.
How many months in a year?
    Twelve, the almanack makes clear.
How many years in an age?
    One hundred, says the sage.
How many ages in time?
    No one knows the rhyme.

PAUL REVERE'S RIDE

Henry W. Longfellow

Listen, my children, and you shall hear
Of the midnight ride of Paul Revere,
On the eighteenth of April, in Seventy-five;
Hardly a man is now alive
Who remembers that famous day and year.

He said to his friend, "If the British march
By land or sea from the town tonight,
Hang a lantern aloft in the belfry arch
Of the North Church tower, as a signal light,—
One, if by land, and two, if by sea;
And I on the opposite shore will be,
Ready to ride and spread the alarm
Through every Middlesex village and farm,
For the country folk to be up and to arm."

Then he said, "Good-night"; and with muffled oar

Silently rowed to the Charlestown shore,
Just as the moon rose over the bay,
Where, swinging wide at her moorings, lay
The Somerset, British man-of-war,
A phantom ship, with each mast and spar
Across the moon like a prison bar,
And a huge black hulk, that was magnified
By its own reflection in the tide.

Meanwhile, his friend through alley and street
Wanders and watches with eager ears,
Till, in the silence around him, he hears
The muster of men at the barrack door,
The sound of arms, and the tramp of feet,
And the measured tread of the grenadiers
Marching down to their boats on the shore.

Then he climbed to the tower of the old North Church,
By the wooden stairs, with stealthy tread,
To the belfry chamber overhead,
And startled the pigeons from their perch
On the sombre rafters, that round him made
Masses and moving shapes of shade;
By the trembling ladder, steep and tall,

To the highest window in the wall,
Where he paused to listen, and look down
A moment on the roofs of the town,
And the moonlight flowing over all.

Beneath, in the churchyard, lay the dead
In their night encampment on the hill,
Wrapped in silence so deep and still
That he could hear, like a sentinel's tread,
The watchful night wind, as it went,
Creeping along from tent to tent,
And seeming to whisper, "All is well!"
A moment only he feels the spell
Of the place and hour, and the secret dread
Of the lonely belfry and the dead,
For suddenly all his thoughts are bent
On a shadowy something far away,
Where the river widens to meet the bay,
A line of black, that bends and floats
On the rising tide, like a bridge of boats.
Meanwhile, impatient to mount and ride,
Booted and spurred, with a heavy stride
On the opposite shore walked Paul Revere.
Now he patted his horse's side,

Now gazed on the landscape far and near,
Then impetuous stamped the earth,
And turned and tightened his saddle girth;
But mostly he watched with eager search
The belfry tower of the old North Church,
As it rose above the graves on the hill,
Lonely and spectral, and sombre and still.
And lo! as he looks, on the belfry's height
A glimmer, and then a gleam of light!
He springs to the saddle, the bridle he turns,
But lingers and gazes, till full on his sight
A second lamp in the belfry burns.

A harry of hoofs in a village street,
A shape in the moonlight, a bulk in the dark,
And beneath from the pebbles, in passing, a spark
Struck out by a steed flying fearless and fleet;
That was all! And yet, through the gloom and the light,
The fate of a nation was riding that night;
And the spark struck out by that steed, in his flight,
Kindled the land into flame with its heat.
He has left the village and mounted the steep,
And beneath him, tranquil and broad and deep,
Is the Mystic, meeting the ocean tides;

And under the alders, that skirt its edge,
Now soft on the sand, now loud on the ledge,
Is heard the tramp of his steed as he rides.

It was twelve by the village clock
When he crossed the bridge into Medford town.
He heard the crowing of the cock,
And the barking of the farmer's dog,
And felt the damp of the river fog,
That rises after the sun goes down.

It was one by the village clock
When he galloped into Lexington,
He saw the gilded weathercock
Swim in the moonlight as he passed,
And the meeting house windows, blank and bare,
Gaze at him with a spectral glare
As if they already stood aghast
At the bloody work they would look upon.

It was two by the village clock
When he came to the bridge in Concord town.
He heard the bleating of the flock,

And the twittering of birds among the trees,
And felt the breath of the morning breeze
Blowing over the meadows brown.
And one was safe and asleep in his bed
Who at the bridge would be first to fall,
Who that day would be lying dead,
Pierced by a British musket ball.
You know the rest. In the books you have read

How the British regulars fired and fled—
How the farmers gave them ball for ball,
From behind each fence and farmyard wall,
Chasing the red coats down the lane,
Then crossing the fields to emerge again
Under the trees at the turn of the road,
And only pausing to fire and load.

So through the night rode Paul Revere;
And so through the night went his cry of alarm
To every Middlesex village and farm—
A cry of defiance, and not of fear—
A voice in the darkness, a knock at the door,
And a word that shall echo forever-more;

For borne on the night wind of the past,

Through all our history to the last,

In the hour of darkness and peril and need,

The people will waken and listen to hear

The hurrying hoof beats of that steed,

And the midnight message of Paul Revere.

LADY MOON

Lord Houghton

———

"Lady Moon, Lady Moon, where are you roving?"
    "Over the sea."
"Lady Moon, Lady Moon, whom are you loving?"
    "All that love me."

"Are you not tired with rolling and never
    Resting to sleep?
Why look so pale and so sad, as for ever
    Wishing to weep?"

"Ask me not this, little child, if you love me;
    You are too bold
I must obey my dear Father above me,
    And do as I'm told."

"Lady Moon, Lady Moon, where are you roving?"
    "Over the sea."
"Lady Moon, Lady Moon, whom are you loving?"
    "All that love me."

Printed in the United States
by Baker & Taylor Publisher Services